I084406I

The Linux Renaissance

Commands and Customization Tips

Table of Contents

Chapter 1. Introduction

Delving into the intricacies of an operating system as rich as Linux can seem daunting, but it no longer needs to be! Welcome to our Special Report: "The Linux Renaissance: Commands and Customization Tips." This comprehensive report is designed from the ground up to demystify the Linux command line environment and provide users with a hands-on guide to customizing Linux to suit their needs. Whether you're an IT professional looking to hone your skills, or a hobbyist entering the realm of Linux for the first time, this report presents this highly technical topic in a conservative and down-to-earth manner. It's time to take the reins of Linux and have the system function in the exact way you prefer; it's time for the Linux Renaissance.

Chapter 2. Understanding the Linux Command Line Interface

Linux is often categorized as a command line-based operating system, and while it is certainly capable of supporting a variety of graphical user environments, it is through the command line interface (CLI) where its true power unfolds. To start, let's consider the basics of how the Linux command line works.

2.1. Introduction to the Linux Command Line Interface

The command line interface, also known as the terminal or shell, is where you type in commands for Linux to execute. A shell is an interpreter of command lines that provides an interface layer between the user and the system. The most widely used shell on Linux is called Bash (Bourne Again Shell). If you are using a Linux system, you are likely working within a Bash shell unless you have consciously chosen an alternative.

Entering a command into the terminal and pressing enter prompts the shell to interpret the command and initiate necessary actions. It's a powerful interaction that bypasses mouse clicks and screen transitions to achieve direct, efficient system operation.

2.2. Basic Terminal Commands

Now let's jump into a few of the most basic and most essential Linux commands.

To check your current directory, use the pwd command, which stands for "Print Working Directory".

```
$ pwd
/home/username
```

Listing directory contents is done with the `ls` command. Typing `ls` and pressing enter will return a list of files and directories in your current location.

To navigate between directories, use the `cd` command. For instance, if you want to move into a directory named 'Documents,' you would type `cd Documents` and press enter.

```
$ cd Documents
```

To create a new empty file, use the `touch` command followed by the name of the file.

```
$ touch newfile.txt
```

Removing a file can be done with the `rm` command, short for remove.

```
$ rm newfile.txt
```

2.3. Command Syntax

Now, you might be wondering how these commands are organized. Linux commands generally adhere to the following format: `command -options arguments`. The command is the action you want executed, the options modify the behavior of the command, and the arguments are the things you want the action to be performed on. The options are usually preceded by a dash (-). Let's take the `ls` command we discussed earlier for an example:

```
$ ls -l /home/username
```

In this example, `ls` is the command, `-l` is the option that lists files in 'long format', and `/home/username` is the argument specifying the directory you want to list.

2.4. Advanced Commands and Techniques

While the basics can get you quite far, Linux is known for its versatility and depth. Thus, the ability to utilize a more extensive selection of commands and techniques is sure to come in handy. Here are a few examples:

The `grep` command has exceptional utility for searching through text files. If you want to check if a specific word or phrase exists within a document, this tool is indispensable.

```
$ grep "specific word" file.txt
```

`chmod` and `chown` are essential for managing file permissions and ownership, a critical part of Linux's robust security model.

```
$ chmod 755 file.txt
$ chown user:group file.txt
```

Standing for "stream editor", the `sed` command enables quick and powerful text transformations.

```
$ sed 's/foo/bar/g' file.txt
```

Finally, it's valuable to realize that any command line operation can be automated via scripting — a topic vast enough to justify its own chapter!

All told, the Linux CLI is less a rote interface and more a vast, interactive playground. As you deepen your understanding of this realm, you'll find that the shell is expansive and conducive to virtually any degree of customization.

2.5. Conclusion

Embedded in the DNA of Linux is the command line interface, holding a myriad of commands and scripting capabilities. While understanding the CLI does require an investment of time and patience, the results are highly rewarding — profound control and efficiency await you.

Throughout this chapter, a broad landscape has been explored — a journey from the simplest commands to more complex actions. However, the CLI is a deep well and learning is a process. As you continue to master the terminal, you will find your path. Remember, 'man' is your friend. When in doubt, `man command` can be your compass amid the sea of possibilities, providing detailed manual pages for virtually every command on your system.

In the world of Linux, the command line interface is not just a tool — it's a gateway to a realm of unlimited possibilities. Whether you're using it for system administration, programming, network management or troubleshooting, the shell offers unparalleled flexibility and power. Welcome to the Linux Renaissance.

Chapter 3. Linux File System: A Comprehensive Overview

The Linux file system can be likened to the central nervous system of the entire operating system; it's the framework that houses all your files and directories. Understanding how it works will empower you to manage and navigate its intricate structure efficiently.

3.1. The File System Hierarchy

Linux bases its file system on a hierarchical structure. At the very top of this hierarchy, you'll find the root directory, represented by a forward slash (/). From the root, branches extend to house different categories of file systems, from system files to user files, each with its own subset of directories.

Below are some of the primary directories you'll find under the root directory:

- /bin: short for binaries; contains basic commands and utilities.

- /boot: contains files necessary for booting the system.

- /dev: short for devices; handles pseudo-devices such as your keyboard or mouse.

- /etc: contains configuration and administrative files.

- /home: home directories for users to store personal files.

- /usr: universal system resources; contains shareable, read-only data.

- /var: variable data files such as logs and databases.

3.2. Understanding Files and Directories

Every file and directory possesses properties that identify and determine its attributes. Running `ls -l` in a directory on the command line will reveal these properties, including the file type, permissions, instance of links, owner, group, size, and the time of the last modification.

3.3. File Permissions

In Linux, each file and directory has assigned access rights. These are mainly controlled by permissions that allow someone to read (r), write (w), or execute (x) a file or directory.

Permissions are structured into three groups, each representing the user, the group, and others, respectively. The `chmod` command enables the changing of permissions.

3.4. Hard and Symbolic Links

Hard links are a means of creating another name for the same file, without actually duplicating the file. A symbolic link or 'symlink' is a file that links to another file or directory. These two types of links are crucial in Linux file systems, providing flexibility in file and folder manipulation.

3.5. File Partitioning and Mounting

Partitioning divides your disk into different sectors, enabling you to manage your files and directories efficiently. Linux uses the `fdisk` command for partitioning.

After partitioning, you'll have to mount the partitions. Mounting makes the file systems available for use. This action assigns a mount point (a directory in existing file system) to the device.

3.6. Tips to Efficiently Navigate the File System

Getting comfortable with Linux's file structure will maximize your productivity. Below are few tricks to remember when navigating:

- Use tab completion: pressing 'tab' will auto-complete file and directory names.

- Use relative and absolute paths efficiently.

- Memorize common commands, such as `ls`, `cd`, `pwd` etc.

In essence, the Linux file system is a rigorous and efficient structure that accommodates all file management needs. Grasping its fundamentals and subtleties can greatly enhance your Linux experience, whether you're a hobbyist or professional. This knowledge equates to mastery – a key tenet of the Linux Renaissance.

Remember, the power of Linux is in its flexibility, versatility, and user control; and therein lies its beauty. Its mechanism encourages exploration and customization while maintaining a robust structure to ensure seamless functionality. Welcome to the Linux Renaissance, your journey into developing skills that empower you to take your Linux systems just where you wish!

Chapter 4. Mastering Basic Linux Commands

Commands constitute the bedrock of the Linux environment, enabling interaction with the system directly, which is both flexible and powerful. Throughout this chapter, we will examine the most essential Linux commands, their functions, and usage.

4.1. The Linux Command Line

The Linux command line, also known as shell, is a text interface for your operating system. It allows you to instruct your computer by inputting commands directly. One of the most common shells in Linux is the Bash (Bourne Again SHell).

To begin, open a terminal window. The terminal is where you will enter your Linux commands. The command prompt usually contains your username, the hostname of your machine, and your current directory or file path. It might resemble this:

```
user@hostname:~$
```

Once the terminal is open, you're ready to start entering commands!

4.2. Basic File System Navigation Commands

Learning how to navigate the file system effectively is crucial when mastering Linux commands.

Present Working Directory (pwd)

Firstly, the 'pwd' command, which stands for "Print Working Directory," is used to display the current directory you are in. This can be seen as your location in the file system.

For example:

```
$ pwd
```

It might output:

```
/home/user
```

List and View Directory Contents (ls)

Next, the 'ls' command, similar to the dir command in Windows CMD, lists the contents of a directory.

For instance, to list your directory's contents:

```
$ ls
```

If the current directory is your home directory, it might output:

```
`Desktop Documents Downloads Music Pictures Videos
```

The 'ls' command has various options which can be used to get more detailed information. Use 'ls -l' to get a long listing of details, including permissions, ownership, size, and modification time.

Change Directory (cd)

The 'cd' command, which stands for "Change Directory," allows you to move between file directories.

To change to a different directory:

```
$ cd directoryname
```

Replace 'directoryname' with the target directory's name.

Clear Terminal (clear)

After executing many commands, the screen can become cluttered.

To clear the screen and have a fresh terminal, use the 'clear' command:

```
$ clear
```

4.3. File Operations

Being able to manipulate files in Linux is another fundamental skill.

1. Creating Files

To create a file in Linux, use the 'touch' command followed by the name of the file:

```
$ touch filename
```

Replace 'filename' with your desired file name.

1. View File Contents (cat)

The 'cat' (short for "concatenate") command is used to view the contents of a file. For example, to view a file named file1.txt, you would type:

```
$ cat file1.txt
```

If file1.txt contained "Hello, world!", the terminal would output:

Hello, world!

1. Copying Files

The 'cp' command allows you to copy files from one location to another.

```
$ cp source destination
```

Replace 'source' with the file to be copied and 'destination' with the location you wish to copy the file to.

1. Move and Rename Files

Moving and renaming files is achieved through the 'mv' command.

```
$ mv oldname newname
```

Replace 'oldname' with the current name and 'newname' with the new name or location.

1. Delete Files

Deleting files in Linux is done using the 'rm' command.

```
$ rm filename
```

Replace 'filename' with the name of the file you desire to delete.

4.4. Processes and System Monitoring

Linux commands are also useful in monitoring your system.

Top

The 'top' command provides you with a dynamic view of the processes running on your system.

```
$ top
```

Uptime

The 'uptime' command lets you see how long your system has been running.

```
$ uptime
```

Free

The 'free' command allows you to check the amount of free and used memory on your system.

This is just the tip of the iceberg! As you delve deeper and practice more with Linux commands, you'll find your proficiency and efficiency improving. Being proficient in commanding Linux could open doors for advanced system administration, scripting, and even kernel development!

Chapter 5. Advanced Linux Commands for Power Users

Command line navigation and operations form the basics of Linux interaction. Our journey has so far covered these foundational aspects, the very skeleton of Linux interaction. However, to truly take command of your Linux system, you need to wield the power of its higher-level commands. They allow you to manipulate system settings, diagnose network issues, manage processes, compare files, and much more. Let this be your initiation into the league of power users.

5.1. Understanding System Processes

Before we can manage system processes, we first need to understand them. Processes in Linux, sometimes referred to as jobs, are instances of running programs. The `ps` command lists these processes.

Here's a common usage of the ps command:

```
ps aux
```

This command lists all system processes. The "a" option tells ps to list the processes of all users on the system. The "u" option tells it to display the process's user/owner, and "x" tells ps to also show processes not attached to a terminal.

5.2. Managing System Processes

The `top` command gives a real-time, dynamic view of the processes running in the system.

```
top
```

This command opens an interactive command line application that displays a real-time view of the processes running on your system. You can exit the top command by simply pressing "q".

5.3. Diagnosing Network Problems

There are a host of Linux commands designed to help you understand and diagnose network problems. A common one is `ping`, which checks the network connectivity.

```
ping example.com
```

This will send a network request to "example.com" and give you a report on how long the response took.

Another useful command is `netstat`, which displays network connections, routing tables, and a number of network interfaces.

```
netstat -rn
```

The "-rn" option instructs netstat to show numerical addresses (as opposed to trying to resolve domain names) and to not attempt to resolve symbolic link names for hosts.

5.4. The Power of the 'grep' Command

The grep command is one of the most useful and versatile commands in a Linux system. Use it to search for a specific string of text in a given input.

```
grep "search term" filename
```

This command will look for the string "search term" within the file named "filename". The grep command can also be used with other commands by piping the output of one into grep.

For example:

```
ls -l | grep "search term"
```

This command will list all files in long format and then search the output for "search term".

5.5. Comparing Files with 'diff'

The diff command compares two files line by line. Let's say we have two files, file1 and file2. Here's how you can compare them:

```
diff file1 file2
```

The output will list the lines that are different. If a line is present in file1 but not in file2, it'll signify as <, and if a line is present in file2 but not in file1, it'll signify as >.

5.6. The Power of Redirection and Pipes

Bash provides the marvels of redirection and pipes allowing you to control inputs and outputs of a command or sequence of commands. The > character is used for redirecting output. The | character, on the other hand, is an incredibly powerful tool that allows you to pipe the output of one command to the input of another.

For instance, to create a text file with the list of all files in a directory:

```
ls > file-list.txt
```

The `ls` command's output is directed into file-list.txt.

To use `grep` to filter output of `ls`:

```
ls | grep ".txt"
```

This will output only the text files in the directory.

5.7. Vim: An Advanced Text Editor

When it comes to text editors in Linux, Vim stands out. It's highly configurable and built for efficiency. To open a file with Vim:

```
vim filename
```

To exit insert mode and command mode:

- Insert mode: Press Esc

- Command mode: Type `:q!` and press enter to exit without saving, `:wq` to save and exit.

5.8. File Permissions

Linux is a multi-user system. File permissions ensure that only authorized individuals can access, modify, or execute your files. Use `ls -l` to view your files & their permissions. The `chmod` command modifies file permissions.

An example:

```
chmod 754 filename
```

This sets the permissions as - the owner can read, write and execute (7), the group can read and execute (5), and others can read only (4).

These advanced commands are just a peek into the power and flexibility that Linux has to offer. Practice each aspect with diligence, and you will inevitably master the art of control, joining the Linux renaissance as proficient power users. Remember, every commendable edifice starts with a single block, and every Linux maestro starts with a command.

Chapter 6. System Administration Basics on Linux

The first step in navigating the course towards becoming a proficient Linux administrator leans heavily on understanding the fundamental concepts related to the role. Management, maintenance, and provision of technical support are a few responsibilities paired with system administration.

6.1. Understanding System Architecture

The building block of Linux system administration is realizing how the system architecture is structured. Every Linux system composes a hierarchy of directories that form the file system. Among these directories, there exists a variety, each performing different functions.

1. `/bin`: It houses essential command binaries that need to be available in single user mode. Examples include: ls, cp, cat, rm.

2. `/etc`: A directory for host-specific system configuration files for the system.

3. `/dev`: Contains device files. For example, tty1, sda1, lp0.

4. `/home`: Home directories for all users to store their personal files.

5. `/opt`: It is reserved for all the software and add-on packages that are not part of the default installation.

6. `/tmp`: Directory that is used by the system to store temporary files. The content gets deleted after a reboot.

The understanding of this structure allows an administrator to navigate, locate, and manage files in a Linux system effectively.

6.2. User and Group Management

User and group management form the core of a Linux system administration role. The two major components associated with this are account management and permissions/security management.

Initially, the focus should be on creating, deleting, and managing users and groups. Linux uses a variety of command line tools for that:

For users; adduser, useradd, userdel, usermod, etc. And for groups; groupadd, groupdel, groupmod, gpasswd, etc.

Before doing that, remember that each user has a unique user ID (UID) and group ID (GID). Users belong to at least one group (the primary group), but they can also belong to numerous other supplementary groups.

Another important concept is that of 'root' (the superuser) and sudo users. The 'root' user has unrestricted access to manage the system, similar to the administrator account on a Windows machine. 'Sudo' users are regular users granted specific (or unlimited) system management rights.

6.3. File Permissions and Ownership

File permissions and ownership determine who can access or manipulate files and directories within a Linux system. Linux supports three types of permissions:

1. Read (r): Permission to read the content of a file or list the contents of a directory.

2. `Write (w)`: Permission to modify the contents of a file or add/remove files in a directory.

3. `Execute (x)`: Permission to run a file or traverse a directory.

File permissions may apply to the user who owns the file/directory (User), to members of the file's owning group (Group), or to other users not in the file's owning group (Other).

The ownership and permission of any file or directory can be changed using commands like "chown", "chgrp", "chmod".

6.4. Working with the Command Line

The foundational part of controlling Linux is mastering the command line. Familiarity with the command line offers a level of power and flexibility over the system that is typically unreachable with graphical interfaces. Commonly used commands that need to be familiar to a system administrator include:

1. File operations: `cp` (copy), `mv` (move), `rm` (remove), `touch` (create a new empty file), `cat` (print file content).

2. Text search: `grep`

3. File permissions and ownership: `chmod`, `chown`

4. Network operations: `ping`, `netstat`, `ssh`, `scp`

5. Process management: `ps`, `top`, `kill`

6. Package management: `apt-get`, `apt-cache` (for systems using Debian-based package management)

7. Disk space: `df`, `du`

8. System info: `uname`, `hostname`

9. Shutdown and reboot: `shutdown`, `reboot`

6.5. Packaging and Installation of Software

Linux permits users to choose from among numerous options for installed software. Precompiled binary packages and compiling your own from the source code are the two primary methods of software installation.

Majority distributions will either use `dpkg` and `apt`, `{rpm}` and `yum`, or `zypper` as their package managers.

These package managers work with repositories or digital locations used for storing and distributing applications. They're automatically connectable and help users find, install, update, and uninstall software packages in an efficient way.

In conclusion, the underlying basics of Linux system administration revolve around understanding system architecture, effectively managing users and groups, setting file permissions and ownership, working with the command line, and handling software packaging and installation. A grasp of these areas is crucial for developing efficient, productive Linux system administration skills. This knowledge, coupled with practical experience, can help foster a viable career or hobby in Linux system administration, thus truly embracing the spirit of the Linux Renaissance.

Chapter 7. Linux Network Configuration and Troubleshooting

Networking in a Linux environment consists of numerous elements, including interfaces, protocols, services, and commands, each contributing to the efficient communication of data between systems. It's important that you understand these fundamentals to be able to configure and troubleshoot the system effectively.

7.1. Understanding Network Interfaces

A network interface represents your system's connection point to a network. It can either be a physical component (like a wired Ethernet or Wireless network card) or a software-created virtual interface (like loopback interface lo).

To view network interfaces on your Linux system, you can use the 'ip' command:

```
$ ip addr show
```

Let's explain some key terminologies in the 'ip addr show' output.

1. 'lo' refers to the loopback interface, enabling the system to send and receive data to/from itself.

2. 'eth0' or 'ens33' may represent your Ethernet (wired) network interface.

3. 'wlan0' or 'wlp3s0' might represent a wireless network interface.

7.2. Network Configuration Files

While you can use commands to manipulate network interfaces directly, the settings will be lost after a reboot unless they're enshrined in configuration files. In Debian-based systems (such as Ubuntu), these settings are contained in /etc/network/interfaces. In Red Hat-based systems, such as CentOS or Fedora, individual config files exist for each interface in /etc/sysconfig/network-scripts/.

```
# Debian-based Systems
$ nano /etc/network/interfaces

# Red Hat-based Systems
$ nano /etc/sysconfig/network-scripts/ifcfg-eth0
```

It's important to reserve changes to configuration files for stable, long-term networking changes.

7.3. Configuring Static IP Addresses

Having a static IP address can be vital for services that require a consistent address, such as servers. You can achieve this by editing the aforementioned network configuration files.

On a Debian-based system, your configuration file might look something like this:

```
auto eth0
iface eth0 inet static
address 192.168.1.2
netmask 255.255.255.0
gateway 192.168.1.254
```

On a Red Hat-based system:

```
DEVICE=eth0
BOOTPROTO=static
ONBOOT=yes
IPADDR=192.168.1.2
NETMASK=255.255.255.0
GATEWAY=192.168.1.254
```

7.4. Troubleshooting Network Issues

No system is perfect, and issues can arise due to misconfigurations, hardware problems, or networking outages.

The 'ping' command is the first step to any network troubleshooting process. With it, you can check if a specific IP address or domain is reachable.

```
$ ping google.com
```

If you're unable to connect to an external site, but can connect to local network resources, your issue might relate to DNS settings or your internet service provider. The file that handles DNS servers on Linux is /etc/resolv.conf.

```
$ nano /etc/resolv.conf
```

If the issue has to do with your internal networking (unable to connect to servers on your local network), it might be due to misconfigured interface settings. Validate your settings by looking at /etc/network/interfaces (Debian-based systems) or /etc/sysconfig/network-scripts/ifcfg-{interface name} (Red Hat-based systems).

Learning to read and understand logs is also part of troubleshooting network issues. The 'dmesg' and 'journalctl' commands help monitor system logs and diagnose potential problems.

```
$ dmesg | grep eth0
$ journalctl -u networking.service
```

In summary, knowledge of the network interfaces, configuration files, IP settings, troubleshooting tools, and several commands is critical in managing and troubleshooting Linux networking. It's a vast field with numerous niche areas, but with regular practice and experience, mastering the topic is feasible. Happy networking in the Linux renaissance!

Chapter 8. Hands-on with Linux Shell Scripting

Before diving headlong into Linux shell scripting, let's get to grips with what a shell script is. A shell script is essentially a series of commands written in a file that the shell can execute. Scripting permits automation of repetitive tasks, management of system jobs, and even the creation of a set of advanced filters or new utilities. It is an indispensable tool in the Linux environment. We shall cover shell basics, control flow, and variables, moving forward into the realms of scripting prowess like conditional statements, loops, and functions.

8.1. What is a Shell?

At its heart, the shell in Linux is a command-line interpreter; it translates the commands typed by the user into operations that the computer's OS can understand. There's a host of shells available in Linux, such as the Bourne Shell (sh), Korn Shell (ksh), C Shell (csh), the highly popular Bourne Again Shell (bash), among others. In this section, though, we are largely going to focus on bash for its extensive functionality and ubiquity. Bash allows command-line editing, unlimited size command history, and job control while still maintaining the basic sh features.

8.2. Basic Shell Scripting

Creating your first shell script needn't be overly complex. Start with opening a text editor, say, vim or nano. Write the following in the first line: `!/bin/bash` The first line of the script is known as a shebang (`!`). It is followed by the path to the interpreter. In this case, `/bin/bash` points towards the bash shell. Following that, a simple `echo` statement will do:

```bash
#!/bin/bash
echo "Hello, Linux world!"
```

Save the above two lines in a file named `hello_world.sh`. Now, before we run the script, it needs to be made executable with `chmod +x hello_world.sh`. Finally, run the script with `./hello_world.sh` and it should print `Hello, Linux world!`

8.3. Variables in Shell Scripting

Bash scripting allows variables. To assign a value to a variable, use "=", with no spaces between the variable, equals sign and the value e.g., `VAR="Hello, Linux world!"` Variables can be accessed using a dollar symbol, such as `echo $VAR`.

8.4. Control Flow: Conditional Statements

Like many programming and scripting languages, bash supports conditional statements. If-then statements, for example, are an essential part of bash scripting:

```bash
#!/bin/bash
if [ -f "/etc/passwd" ]
then
    echo "Your file exists;"
fi
```

Here '-f' checks if "/etc/passwd" exists and is a regular file. If the statement is true, it prints "Your file exists." The shell provides several other such options making script writing extremely versatile, `-d`, for instance, checks for a directory.

8.5. Control Flow: Loops

In addition to conditional statements, loops form a fundamental aspect of control structures in bash scripting. Three types of loops are used commonly: for, while, and until.

A simple demonstration of a for loop is:

```
#!/bin/bash
for i in 1 2 3 4 5
do
   echo "Welcome $i times"
done
```

A while loop example:

```
#!/bin/bash
count=1
while [ $count -le 5 ]
do
   echo "Welcome $count times"
   count=$(( count+1 ))
done
```

An until loop works essentially as a reversed while loop:

```
#!/bin/bash
count=1
until [ $count -gt 5 ]
do
   echo "Welcome $count times"
   count=$(( count+1 ))
```

```
done
```

8.6. Advanced Shell Scripting: Functions

Functions are a convenient way to group commands for execution as a single unit. Here is an example of a bash script using a function:

```
#!/bin/bash
print_hello_world() {
  echo "Hello, Linux world!"
}
print_hello_world
```

As is evident, the function `print_hello_world` is defined at the start and called later. It encapsulates the `echo` command and executes it when called.

8.7. Working with Arguments

Shell scripts can process command-line arguments, providing more flexibility and interactive capabilities to scripts. Arguments are supplied to scripts through positional parameters, accessed with special shell variables.

```
#!/bin/bash
echo "The script name: $0"
echo "The first argument: $1"
echo "The second argument: $2"
```

In the script above, $0 holds the script name, serving handy when debugging. $1 and $2 access the first two arguments given to the script, sequentially. $@ refers to all parameters and $# returns the count of total parameters.

Shell scripting with Linux can be an intriguing, challenging yet rewarding journey. We've scratched the surface here; however, there's much more, from process management to script debugging to explore. A strong grasp of shell scripting paves the way for efficient Linux use, aiding automation, and reducing dependence on manual interaction. Happy scripting in the Linux Renaissance!

Chapter 9. Essential Linux System Monitoring and Performance Tuning Techniques

System monitoring and performance tuning are arguably among the most crucial aspects of managing any operating system, particularly Linux. Responsiveness, availability, and stability of a system can all be attributed to the proper monitoring and tuning practices you adopt. This section walks you through some of the essential Linux system monitoring and performance tuning techniques.

9.1. Understanding System Load

Linux system load represents the number of tasks that are currently waiting for CPU time. System load can offer a quick snapshot of what's happening on your server at any given moment. Three numbers often represent it; load average over the last 1, 5, and 15 minutes. You can use the `uptime` or `w` command to get the system load:

```
$ uptime
14:01:09 up 13 days,  3:38,  1 user,  load average:
0.08, 0.24, 0.30
```

In this example, the load average over the last 1 minute is 0.08, over the last 5 minutes is 0.24, and over the last 15 minutes is 0.30. If the one-minute load average is larger than the 15-minutes one, it means that the load is increasing.

9.2. CPU Monitoring

One crucial resource that needs monitoring is the Central Processing Unit (CPU). top is a real-time command-line utility in Linux used primarily for monitoring CPU. It provides a live, dynamic view of the processes running on the system.

```
$ top
```

The command will display detailed information, including system uptime, users, load average, and top processes using the CPU.

9.3. Memory Monitoring

Closely monitoring memory usage can help prevent a situation where your server runs out of memory, leading to system crashes or slowdowns. The free command is a simple and easy way to keep an eye on memory usage:

```
$ free -h
```

The -h option displays memory statistics in human-readable format.

9.4. Disk Usage Monitoring

Disk usage is another area that needs keen monitoring. Over time, files and directories can take up substantial disk space. The du and df commands allow you to monitor the use of disk space.

```
$ df -h
```

The `-h` option displays the disk usage summary in a human-readable format.

9.5. Network Traffic Monitoring

Monitoring network traffic is essential for diagnosing network issues and detecting network intrusion attempts. The `iftop` command monitors network interface bandwidth usage in real-time:

```
$ iftop
```

9.6. Linux Performance Tuning

With a good grasp of system monitoring, it becomes easier to tune your Linux system for optimal performance. The primary areas we can adjust include the CPU, memory, disk I/O, and network.

9.7. CPU Performance Tuning

In Linux, usual tools for CPU performance tuning are `nice` and `renice` commands. They allow you to influence the CPU scheduler to favor or disfavor certain processes.

```
$ nice -n 10 big_cpu_user_process
```

In the above example, the command `nice -n 10` runs `big_cpu_user_process` with a lower CPU priority.

9.8. Memory Performance Tuning

Memory performance tuning revolves around controlling how Linux uses system memory. The `sysctl` command can be used to modify kernel parameters at runtime:

```
$ sysctl vm.swappiness=10
```

The command above adjusts the `vm.swappiness` kernel parameter, which controls the tendency of the kernel to move processes out of physical memory to the swap space.

9.9. Disk I/O Performance Tuning

Improving Disk I/O performance can often be achieved using the `hdparm` utility:

```
$ hdparm -tT /dev/sda1
```

The `-tT` options measure the reading speed of the disk.

9.10. Network Performance Tuning

`ethtool` is a standard Linux utility for controlling network drivers and hardware:

```
$ ethtool -G eth0 rx 4096 tx 4096
```

This command sets the RX and TX buffer sizes for `eth0`.

Remember, performance tuning should be done with care. It's essential to monitor the impact of changes you make to understand their impact and be ready to revert them if they do not produce desired results. Above all, always ensure that these actions align with your organization's operations and strategic objectives to avoid causing disruptions. Each system is unique, so it is crucial to formulate a solution that promotes this uniqueness. Welcome to the Linux renaissance, the era of profound system understanding and customization!

Chapter 10. Customizing Your Linux: Personalization and Theming

Personalization offers a way to give your Linux interface your unique touch. From changing your desktop wallpaper, altering icon packs, adjusting window managers to tweaking the shell prompt, an abundance of options exist to customize your Linux.

10.1. Getting Acquainted with Linux Theming

In Linux, you can choose from hundreds of open-source themes available to make your system look and feel the way you want. This can revolve around subtle visual tweaks or complete visual overhauls. To start with, you will want to be familiar with the elements you can change:

1. **Desktop Wallpaper:** Nearly all Linux desktop environments allow customization of the desktop wallpaper. This is usually as easy as right-clicking on the desktop to change it.

2. **Icon Packs:** Icons make up a considerable chunk of your system's visual real estate. An icon set can bring a stark change in your Linux feel.

3. **Window Managers:** In Linux, the window manager is a crucial player in your system's look and feel. It determines window behavior and appearance.

4. **Shell Prompt:** The shell prompt is particularly important for those who spend a lot of time in the terminal. You can change colors, information displayed, and more.

5. **GTK and QT Themes:** Both are widget toolkits used in designing graphical user interfaces.

Let's take a deep dive into each area to uncover how to best curve Linux to your preferences.

10.2. Desktop Wallpaper Customization

Changing your Linux wallpaper is most likely the quickest route to personalizing your environment.

On GNOME desktop, the process is fairly simple. You just need to right-click on an empty area in your desktop and select the "Change Background" option. It should open a settings window, where you can select a wallpaper from the library or add your own.

For KDE plasma desktop, right-clicking anywhere on the desktop will give an option "Configure Desktop and Wallpaper." Here you can select an image of your liking or use the `Get New Wallpapers` button to fetch more.

10.3. Changing Icon Packs

Your Linux distribution will often come with a default set of icons designed to complement its overall look and feel. But you don't have to stick with these. There are countless icon packs available and you can change the icons at will.

The method of installing new icon sets varies based on your chosen desktop environment. If you're a GNOME user, you need an application called `Gnome Tweaks`. Once installed, download your favorite icon pack, extract it in `~/.icons` directory and use `Gnome Tweaks` to apply the new icons.

In KDE Plasma, you need to go to System Settings → Icons → Install from File, and then select your icon pack file to install it. Once done, choose the newly installed pack from the list and click on Apply.

10.4. Window Managers: Another Layer of Personalization

The window manager is what manages your system's windows. It's responsible for the look and placement of windows, which includes the title bar, minimize/maximize/close buttons, window resizing, the border, and more.

In GNOME, you can use the Gnome Tweaks tool to change the window decorations among other settings. While with KDE Plasma, System Settings → Application Style → Window Decorations is where you'll find options for customization.

10.5. Customizing the Shell Prompt

If you're someone that spends a good deal of time on the terminal, the shell prompt offers another customization avenue. You can customize it by altering your ~/.bashrc file (if you're using bash shell) or ~/.zshrc file (if using zsh shell).

Here's a simple example that changes the command prompt to display the current working directory:

```
prompt]# echo 'PS1="\w $ "' >> ~/.bashrc
prompt]# source ~/.bashrc
```

This changes the prompt to your current folder location.

10.6. GTK and QT Themes

Both GTK and QT are widget toolkits used to draw elements. GTK is primarily used by GNOME and GNOME-based desktops, while QT is used by KDE.

To change your GTK theme in GNOME, you need the Gnome Tweaks tool. Navigate to the Appearance section and here under Themes, you can find options to change the GTK theme.

In KDE, elements are drawn using QT. You can install new themes via the System Settings → Appearance → Global Theme → Get New Global Themes option. Once downloaded, they're made available for you to choose straight away.

10.7. Conclusion

The possibilities for customization are immense. You're encouraged to tweak and tune the system until it perfectly fits your workflow and aesthetic tastes. Just remember, every choice you make here is reversible, so don't be afraid to experiment; after all, one of the virtues of the Linux Renaissance is the power of limitless choices it affords its users!

Chapter 11. Securing Your Linux System: Best Practices

Securing your Linux system is of paramount importance, and doing so requires the implementation of several best practices. From ensuring your system is always up-to-date to configuring firewall settings, these practices protect your system from potential threats and enhance its overall security features.

11.1. Up-to-Date System

Ensuring your Linux system is up-to-date is a fundamental first step to securing your system. Updating your system helps to patch known security vulnerabilities.

To update your Linux system, one of the most common commands you'll use is:

```
$ sudo apt-get update && sudo apt-get upgrade
```

This command works on Debian-based systems like Ubuntu and Linux Mint. On a system like Fedora, which uses RPM packages, you would use:

```
$ sudo dnf upgrade
```

11.2. User and Group Management

Managing users and groups effectively is another central aspect of Linux security. Restricting user privileges, creating special-purpose accounts for distinct tasks, and judiciously assigning administrative tasks can significantly decrease the potential for misuse or inadvertent system disruptions.

Creation of a new user can be done using the following command:

```
$ sudo adduser newuser
```

You can add a new group with:

```
$ sudo addgroup newgroup
```

And users can be added to groups as such:

```
$ sudo adduser newuser newgroup
```

11.3. Password Policies

Robust password policies are an integral part of ensuring system security. Ensure that users change their passwords regularly, and are encouraged to use lengthy, complex passwords that are not easy to crack. The PAM (Pluggable Authentication Modules) can help enforce these policies.

You can change a user's password with the passwd command:

```
$ sudo passwd username
```

Implement password aging using the chage command like this:

```
$ sudo chage -M 60 username
```

The above command will force the user to change their password every 60 days.

11.4. Permission Management

Proper file and directory permission management will help prevent unauthorized access to sensitive data. Linux follows a three-tier permission structure: for the 'user', 'group', and 'others'. Permissions include 'read', 'write', and 'execute'.

To change the permissions on a file or directory, we use the chmod command:

```
$ sudo chmod 754 filename
```

In the above example, '7' gives the user full permissions, '5' allows the group to read & execute but not write, and '4' only allows others to read.

11.5. Firewall Configuration

A well-configured firewall can efficiently protect your system from many types of network-based attacks. Tools like 'iptables' or 'ufw' (uncomplicated firewall) can secure your system from undesired connections.

To enable ufw use:

```
$ sudo ufw enable
```

Adding rules can be done like so:

```
$ sudo ufw allow 22/tcp
```

The command above allows tcp connections over port 22, which is the default SSH port.

11.6. Investigating Logs

Keeping a keen eye on system logs can help identify potential security hazards, unusual events, or activities. The 'logwatch' utility is an effective tool for overseeing system logs.

To install logwatch, you can use the command:

```
$ sudo apt-get install logwatch
```

Should you wish to view the logs of a particular service, say SSH, you can use:

```
$ sudo logwatch --service sshd
```

These best practices go a long way in setting up a secure Linux environment. However, no system can be 100% secure. Always treat security as an ongoing process, continually learning, adapting, and implementing safety measures. Always explore new ways to safeguard your system and make security your habit. It is this combination of practices and mindset that will truly stand as your system's most reliable defense.

www.ingramcontent.com/pod-product-compliance
Lightning Source LLC
Chambersburg PA
CBHW071006260726
48661CB00007B/2817